First Team at Cricket

In this series

First Team at Gymnastics

First Team at Football

First Team at Tennis

PETER SACKETT

First Team at Cricket

ILLUSTRATED BY
Mike Francis

DRAGON
Grafton Books

Dragon Books
Grafton Books
A division of the Collins Publishing Group
8 Grafton Street, London W1X 3LA

Published by Dragon Books 1986

This book has been created and produced by
Nomad Publishers Ltd,
The Grange, Grange Yard, London SE1 3AG

ISBN 0-583-30827-9

Printed and bound in Finland

Chapter One

'The plan or not the plan? That is the question!' Pete was having difficulty shaking off the after-effects of his English Literature examination as he addressed himself wholeheartedly to the decision he would soon have to take: a decision that might just make all the difference between glorious victory and abject defeat.

The Plan had come to Pete early that morning while he was still half-asleep in bed. The evening before he had been discussing the big end-of-season game with some of his team mates and somehow his sub-conscious had marshalled all the facts while he'd been fast asleep and come up with a seemingly brilliant solution to win the day. But Pete knew that he had not yet had enough time to examine *The Plan* from every angle. He wanted to satisfy himself that it was thoroughly sound, not just one of those wild, crazy, unworkable ideas that sometimes come to you in the middle of the night.

If Pete adopted *The Plan*, he would be acting completely out of character. This could upset some members of the team who had settled into a good routine during the season and knew, or thought they knew, what to expect from Pete. Would it shake their confidence? Or would it inspire them? Pete wasn't sure. All season he had told his team, Oswestry, to go out there and play their normal game and that approach had worked well. They had had a successful season by any standards: undefeated all summer term, with seven outright victories and the better of three drawn matches. All this had been achieved without recourse to a plan of any kind.

Pete walked to the wicket with the opposition skipper, Adrian Smith. What would Pete do if he won the toss?

'The Plan or not the Plan?' Pete was still undecided and time was running out.

The main problem was Adrian's younger brother, Justin Smith. He had grown the best part of a foot during the winter and had developed from a promising medium-pace bowler to a really quick one — all in the space of one season. Justin's team, Kynaston, relied on him to blast out the opposition, and he rarely failed them. By school standards, Justin was so fast that batting helmets should have been compulsory for the unfortunate few who had to face him at his freshest. It was a common sight all season to see young opening batsmen backing away to square leg instead of getting behind the ball, for the simple reason that they were scared of being hit. Not all school pitches are perfect and Justin's shorter balls, or 'softeners' as he liked to call them, had often set up a juicy victim for him next ball: the short ball, just short of a length, would lift enough to hit the batsman somewhere around the ribs and this would be followed by a 'yorker' of full length which would splatter the unprotected stumps as the batsman backed away anticipating another short ball and another painful blow.

Justin had a mean streak in him and did not mind using it to get the result he wanted!

Pete and Adrian reached the square and examined the prepared batting strip, 22 yards long and 3 yards wide. The wicket was immaculate. Pete pressed his thumb into the heavily rolled surface, around a length. The ground was firm, even hard. This would undoubtedly be a fast but true track, making for an even contest between batsman and bowler in normal circumstances. But today the hard wicket would make Justin a half-metre faster than usual.

Alarm bells rang in Pete's head as he contemplated this fact while tossing a coin high into the air.

'Heads' called Adrian.

The coin, caught in a gusting cross-wind, swirled across the wicket and landed on the edge of the track.

Pete and Adrian shuffled over to the coin and bent to examine it without touching it.

Pete's heart was thumping. This was a toss he badly wanted to win since his plan, if he decided to go through with it, would only work if his side batted first.

'Heads it is!' Adrian was cock-a-hoop.

Pete pressed his thumb into the surface of the batting strip.

A big confident smile spread across his face as Adrian announced his decision a little louder than was necessary.

'We'll put you in!'

Pete was astounded but kept control of his features and remained outwardly calm. The psychological battle had begun.

'Fine! Absolutely fine! I'd have batted anyway. Don't know why we bothered to toss up!'

Pete and Adrian marched back to the pavilion without exchanging another word.

Pete was seething inside.

On a near-perfect wicket like this you should always bat first except in a limited over game, which this certainly wasn't. To be put in on a perfect track was the height of insult. It was like saying to Oswestry 'Look fellows, you are just not good enough to give us a game so let's get this over with quickly shall we and we'll soon be on our way!'

'Right. That's it! *The Plan* it is!'

Pete had not made the carefully considered decision he wanted. A flash of anger and pride had taken control of his thought processes. The gauntlet had been thrown down by Kynaston and he was picking it up, accepting the challenge.

'What are we doing Skip?' shouted Mike 'Spaghetti' Weston, his star opening bat, from the boundary edge before Pete was even half-way back.

It was a little undignified for a captain of his standing to shout back, 'We're batting, get your pads on!' so Pete mimed the action of a straight drive and the pulse rate of the first three in the batting order quickened with the realisation that they would soon be called into action.

His vital decision made, about *The Plan*, Pete allowed himself a brief moment's relaxation as he continued his walk back to the pavilion.

He took a deep breath, slackened the pace of his quick purposeful stride, and savoured his

As he walked back to the pavilion, Pete saw that the ground was filling up with spectators.

favourite scent of all time: the smell of freshly cut grass on the outfield, a smell synonymous in his mind with that glorious game of cricket.

This was the last game of the season so Pete took another deep breath, committing the delicious aroma to memory to see him through the long dark winter months to come.

Pete looked around the ground as he completed his journey back to the pavilion. It was fast filling up with supporters for both teams. This end-of-term clash had developed into a regular fixture between the two rival schools and a tradition had developed that both schools were given a half-day's holiday to watch the game. This was the show-piece of the season and Pete could sense the atmosphere building up.

Neither Shakespeare nor Hamlet would be of any use to him now. The scene was set and soon the characters in this play would take part and events unfold, leaving the audience, Pete hoped, spellbound.

Pete's mind was relaxed and wandered from 'Hamlet' to 'As You Like It':

'All the World's a stage,

And all the men and women merely players', Pete quoted loudly, quite forgetting himself and startling the opposition skipper who raced on ahead giving him a strange sideways look.

'They have their exits and their entrances', Pete continued, feeling closer to Shakespeare than he had all week.

'How very apt' he thought, hoping his

particular exit would be long delayed once he had made his entrance to the wicket.

There was no script but Pete, school captain and master tactition, would at least provide a framework for the day's play. For did he not have a cunningly devised *Plan* with which to win the day?

Pete couldn't guarantee himself a starring role but he would, he hoped, soon be directing events and forcing a satisfactory finale to the day's play — a glorious victory for Oswestry!

Chapter Two

By the time Pete got back to the pavilion the entire Oswestry team had gathered in the changing room, expecting a few words of encouragement from their captain before the game started. They would not be disappointed! Pete intended saying more than just a few words, but first he drew his usual opening partner, Mike, quietly to one side.

'I've decided to put *The Plan* into operation after all so I won't be opening with you today Spaghetti. I'll be going in as number six.'

Mike nodded and swallowed hard. As vice-captain Mike was the only member of the team who knew anything about *The Plan*. Pete had 'phoned him first thing that very morning to get his opinion and Mike had immediately advised against it. In his opinion, *The Plan* was far too risky. Mike was not a typical dour opening batsman and he was not above taking a few risks early in his innings — but what *The Plan* called for was crazy. It was asking a lot of any opening batsman to act against his very nature which was simply, in the first instance, to give his side a safe and steady start.

Pete saw a flicker of doubt cross Mike's eyes but he knew he could count on total support from his best friend. If things didn't go according to plan he would need his vice-captain's help and advice and it was good to know he could count on that.

Pete looked up, taking the whole team into his sights. He paused, waiting for complete attention before speaking, searching individual faces to gauge the mood of his team in order to pitch his speech at the right level.

Every eye was now on the captain. The nervous chatter in the changing room had stopped. There was an expectant hush as Pete jumped onto one of the changing room benches and took up the position at stage centre.

'O.K. team. This is it, the game of our lives. The game we've been preparing for all year!

'The First Team have not lost a game all season and we certainly don't expect to start losing now!

'However, Kynaston are by far the strongest team we've faced so it's not going to be easy. We all want to do well, individually and as a team, so I don't need to psyche you up for this match do I? You know what's at stake and I know you'll do your very best. I hope and trust you all want to win as badly as I do!

'Just in case there's someone in this room that doesn't, let me tell you this: Kynaston are swaggering about as though they have already won the game. Like us they've been unbeaten all season and they aren't even contemplating defeat today. So let's wipe those cocky smiles off their faces as quickly as possible!'

Pete paused, theatrically. His team-mates erupted with released emotion:

'What a nerve!'

'Flipping cheek!'

'Snide lot!'

'Who do they think they are?'

Pete paused, waiting for complete attention before he began his speech.

Pete raised a hand to silence the murmerings which were growing louder. The First Team responded immediately. Pete could feel the control he had over his team.

'O.K. team that's enough of that! Let's speak for ourselves on the pitch — action not words is what I'm looking for from you today!

'Now let's be realistic. Kynaston are good. They're not as good as they think they are, but they're good. They'll take a lot of beating and they won't go down without a struggle.

'In my opinion, we've got a better allround team but they have one player who could swing this match their way, and we all know who that is!

'Yes, Justin Smith.

'I won't pretend he isn't fast. I won't give you any false confidence. He's very fast and he could be a match winner if we give him half a chance. But we aren't going to, are we Mike? Are we Beefy?'

Mike and Beefy responded positively, Beefy by flexing his huge muscles in an improvised Mr Universe pose.

An eruption of laughter at Beefy's antics underlined just how tense everyone was feeling.

Pete was careful not to mention that they had been put in to bat. He didn't want his team to know that Kynaston were quite that confident. He continued:

'Our groundsman, Crowbar, has prepared a perfect wicket for us to bat on so Justin can't get up to any of his bodyline stuff on this track.

He'll be fast but true. I think the key to winning this match is how we handle Justin.

'I'm absolutely sure that Kynaston will set an incredibly attacking field to start with. They'll expect our openers to play their usual game of defending carefully, of not taking any chances, of trying to give us a good steady start. So they'll leave lots of gaps in the field while they pack their fielders into catching positions. They'll be expecting to pick up a good few cheap wickets with Justin's thunderbolts while we struggle to defend.'

Pete paused again. This was the moment he had been leading up to. *The Plan* was about to be uncovered. He hoped The First Team would take it well. Pete crossed his fingers behind his back before proceeding.

'Well, I've got a surprise for us all, you and Kynaston, both! We are not going to play our usual game. We are going to take the game to Kynaston and seize the initiative by catching them off guard!

'Spider — I want you to open with Spaghetti today. I know you haven't opened all season. Now's your chance to show us what you can do. I don't want either of you to play like opening batsmen. I don't want either of you to play yourselves in. I want you both to hit the first ball you receive for four. And I want to see you swing the bat at everything.'

Spider Spadcock couldn't believe his ears. He was one of Oswestry's fast bowlers and was sometimes promoted in the batting order when quick runs were wanted — but to be asked to open in such an important match. . .

Pete had not finished.

'Simon — you remain at number three. But no 'posing' today. I know you look beautiful and your shots are beautiful, but there are no photographers around and no prizes for stylish follow-throughs when you should be scampering singles. I want to catch this lot with their pants down. I want to hit them hard and quick, so quick that we'll have 30 runs on the board before they know what's hit them.

'Here's the scenario,' Pete beamed as he used the new word he had recently acquired.

'Our first four batsmen go in like men possessed. Justin roars in expecting to frighten you and gets the fright of his own life instead! We hook him, edge him over slips, take suicidal runs and generally get away with murder. Justin's got a very short fuse — he's even rattier than you Spider! — and he's furious. The more he's hit, the madder he gets and the faster and wilder he bowls. We take him to the cleaners even though we lose wickets along the way! Beefy comes in at number 5, presses home our advantage and destroys a despondent Kynaston with a devastating Botham-type innings and we've as good as got the game in the bag by tea-time!'

Pete sounded convincing. His enthusiasm spread around the room and was reflected back by way of yells of delight. It looked as though *The Plan* had been well received!

'However,' Pete dropped his voice and suddenly sounded dead serious, 'If by any chance we lose three quick wickets I'm going in at number 5 and Beefy at number 6. We'll have to weather the storm and you, Beefy, will have to control yourself and play a responsible innings for once! But I'm sure it won't come to that. We're going to win. And we're going to win in style!

'We're the better team, we're the prettier team — aren't we Poser? — and we deserve to win! So go to it, team! Let's slaughter them!'

The First Team roared in delight. Poser Simon entered into the spirit of things. He shook his blond locks, held his head up high, licked his fingers and brushed back the sides of his hair with them, as if preparing himself for a major television appearance.

Pete had done well in getting his players into the right frame of mind. His job done, Pete turned dramatically on his heels and wheeled out of the changing room into the fresh air outside. He had wound his team up and now he wanted to leave his openers a little time on their own to prepare for the onslaught that was to come.

He did not feel as confident as he had sounded. But he readily accepted responsibility and that's why he enjoyed being captain so even if the worst came to the worst, Pete thought, he'd still be able to cope. He allowed himself a little smile at the thought of putting one across Kynaston as he lent on the pavilion rail and watched the opposition warm up.

Kynaston were loosening up with fielding practice and one boy stood out from the others. He was much taller than his team-mates and had a superior and confident air about him. Pete took an immediate dislike to him.

'That's Justin O.K.' thought Pete. He was surprised at the way he had not only shot up since last season, but had also filled out. His shoulders were broader and he looked a good stone heavier.

Poser Simon shook his blond locks, licked his fingers and brushed back the sides of his hair.

The thought of beating Kynaston made Pete smile as he leant on the pavilion rail and watched them warm up.

Justin limbered up by pretending to be a windmill; his huge arms catherine-wheeled through the air at a great speed of knots.

Someone threw Justin a ball and he began bowling off just three strides to the wicket-keeper, who was the last of the opposition to

The ball thudded into the wicketkeeper's hands.

appear on the field after putting on all his protective gear. The ball thudded into the keeper's hands. Even with his big padded gloves on, the keeper felt the ball bruise his fingers, and he backed away from the bowler as he threw the ball back to him, trying desperately to increase the distance between them before the next practice ball was bowled.

Pete's self-congratulatory smile dissolved; he could hear alarm bells ringing in his head for the second time that day.

The rumours had been true then. Justin was fearsomely fast!!

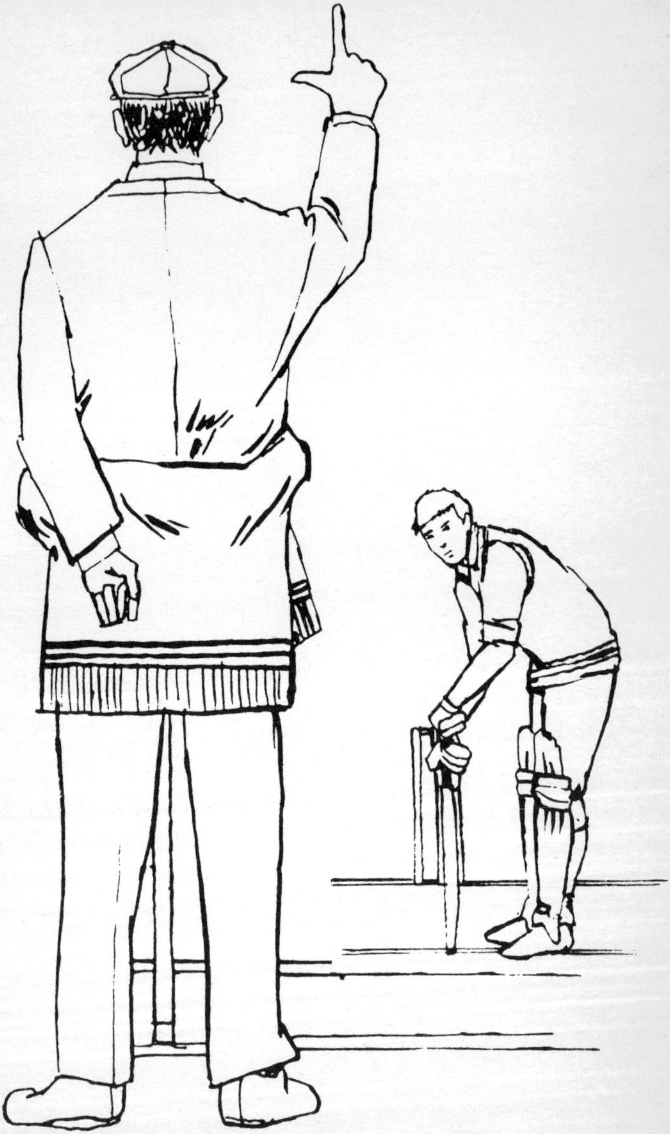

'Middle-and-leg, please umpire,' called Mike.

Chapter Three

'Middle-and-leg please umpire.'

Mike moved his bat sidewards in front of the stumps as the umpire directed him to his chosen guard. He tapped the turf around his crease to mark his guard, simultaneously taking a huge breath and letting the air out slowly in an effort to calm himself down a little. He could feel his excitement mounting, and he did not want the opposition to know that he felt nervous in any way.

Holding his bat off the ground, he surveyed the field placings. The opposition side were all in position. Justin had marked out his run and was ready to start bowling, but Mike took his time, looking carefully at every fielder's position.

His captain, Pete, had been absolutely right: Kynaston had set a ridiculously aggressive field.

There were no less than three slips, a gully,

point and silly-mid-off on the off-side, and three short legs (two backward, one forward) on the on-side. The wicket-keeper and first slip were standing well back and the bowler seemed to be just a speck on the horizon; everyone else was crowding in on him, far too close for comfort.

Mike could feel the opposition getting restless but still he wasn't ready to start. Making

At the start of play the field placings looked like this.

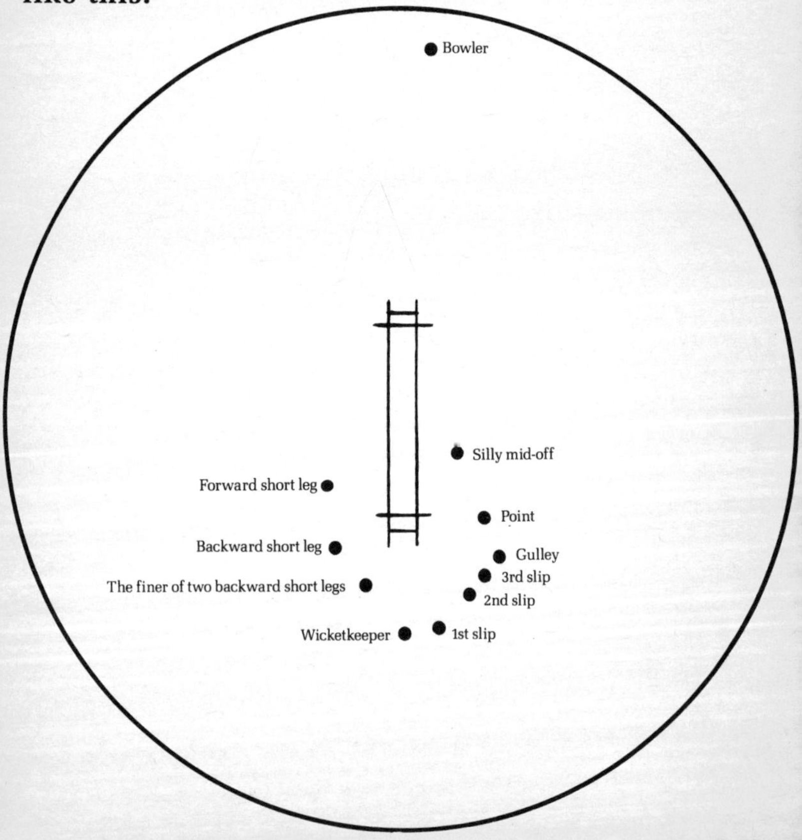

a mental note of every single fielding position, he analysed the gaps in the field that Pete had predicted.

For a start, there was no third man or fine leg, so if he could deflect the ball past the close fielders runs were to be had there.

There was no-one at square leg so anything short could be pulled quite safely.

Most of the area in front of the wicket on both sides of the field was entirely unprotected with no mid-on, no conventional mid-off and no-one in the covers. A firm push, let alone a drive, to anything pitched up would produce runs in front of the wicket.

Mike was now ready to face the first ball, and settled down in a relaxed stance with his feet slightly apart straddling the crease. As Justin roared in he patted the ground behind his back foot with his bat exactly five times. This was his magic formula for warding off bad luck; it gave him the confidence to face every ball and he never faced a ball without going through this routine.

'Play' called the umpire when he was satisfied that everyone including the scorers was ready.

Justin looked mean and hostile and Mike was acutely aware of the intimidating presence of all those hungry hawks hovering around him. Justin seemed to take forever to get to the wicket. Mike's concentration was beginning to slip and nasty pictures were flashing in front of his mind — pictures of shattered stumps and flying bails — not nice pictures at all! Beads of perspiration broke out on his forehead and he suddenly felt weak in all his joints. He felt as though he barely had the strength to lift his bat off the ground, let alone hit the ball off the square!

Justin was four paces away from his final delivery stride and Mike was in entirely the wrong frame of mind. How on earth did Pete expect him to hit the first ball for six; he would be well satisfied to survive it!

The tension was unbelievable and something had to snap.

Forward-short-leg took a sudden pace forward and muttered evilly in Mike's direction,

'Just-in, Just-out!'

It was meant to be a quiet, no doubt pre-planned and well rehearsed, intimidating gesture between fielder and batsman but the atmosphere was so tense that the words came out louder than intended and were clearly audible at twenty paces.

Mike 'Spaghetti' Weston was momentarily distracted and the ball fizzed through his inadequate defences, making *mincemeat* of his stumps.

'Spaghetti Bolognese!' shrieked the keeper.

'Spaghetti *Bowler*-nese!' yelled first slip, improving on the pun.

Both had played against Spaghetti in the *football match between the two schools earlier

* See 'First Team at Football'

that year so both were familiar with his nickname and were revelling in their spontaneous ingenuity.

But their joy was short lived because the umpire, Mr Able, had seen and heard everything. In his younger days he had been a fast bowler of sorts and knew all the tricks. He was unable to stop Justin from bowling but *was* able to shout "Dead Ball!" after the ball had taken its course, indicating his decision to the scorers by criss-crossing his arms in a curious downward, cancelling gesture.

'Dead ball,' called umpire Able, criss-crossing his arms to indicate his decision.

After which all hell seemed to break loose!

Justin's over-zealous follow-through had taken him to within a couple of yards of the batsman's crease and he stood, utterly unbelieving, hands on hips, staring at Spaghetti in demented fashion.

'You jammy devil!' he shouted, making Mike feel totally inadequate. That ball would have beaten Mike with or without short-leg's efforts, as both bowler and batsman well knew.

This was all too much for 'Spider' Spadcock, the other opening batsman. He came charging down the wicket to join in the fracas.

'You little cheats' Spider yelled as he threw himself protectively between batsman and bowler.

Mr Able was quick off the mark. He hurried down the wicket as rapidly as his bulky frame permitted and defused the explosive start to the game.

'Cut that out! We'll have none of that while I'm in charge!' Mr Able spoke with the clear authority of the deputy headmaster that he was. The players responded and reluctantly shuffled away.

The middle stump had been split in half and while the square-leg umpire toddled off to fetch a new one, Mr Able called over Kynaston's skipper, Justin's brother Adrian, for a stern lecture on how cricket should be played, about the true spirit of the game and how he had better start controlling his players or there would be no game that afternoon.

Mike took the opportunity of getting himself together. He strode off to square-leg and thwacked the bat against his pads in an angry gesture. 'You silly fool' he chided himself 'You must think positively! You're as good — no better — than anyone on this field and you *can* take Justin apart.' Mike put his bat on the ground and shook the nervous tension out of his hands as he jogged lightly on the spot with his arms hanging loosely by his sides. He was getting a second chance and he resolved to make the most of it.

'Play,' Mr Able, or Mable as he was affectionately known once his second name initial 'M' had been discovered, waved the game on when everything had settled down.

Once again Justin came tearing in.

This time Mike was ready for him. He was half-expecting an angry, short ball and sure enough a bumper it was. Mike moved inside it and swung his bat aggressively, just as his skipper had asked him to. But the ball ballooned unconvincingly over short-leg and would certainly have been swallowed up by square-leg, had there been one.

Mike and Spider Spadcock scampered two runs and Mike had broken his duck. Justin was not amused. The game had barely started and already Justin was fuming. He snatched at the ball when it was thrown back to him and stomped off to his starting mark on surely the longest run up in school cricket.

The next ball was short again. It wasn't a

bumper and it wasn't a long-hop. But it was considerably short of a length and well outside the off-stump. Justin was trying to bowl too fast too early in his spell and he was sacrificing control for speed. The ball was wide enough for Mike to shoulder arms and let it pass safely through to the wicketkeeper, and that's exactly what he would have done in normal circumstances. But this was not a normal sort of day, far from it. He was under orders to throw the bat at everything, so he did just that.

He slashed horizontally at the ball as it reared up shoulder high. This time he was getting a feel for the pace of the wicket and played his shot with perfect timing. The ball sped high over point's head and incredibly cleared the boundary ropes first bounce.

It wasn't a classic square cut, Mike had made no attempt to get over the ball and keep it down, but the ball had been hit with the full face of the bat and the batsman got a lot of pleasure from striking the ball so sweetly.

Oswestry supporters applauded wildly. 'Good shot, Spaghetti' encouraged Spider as the ball was retrieved from the boundary.

Mike acknowledged the praise by smiling modestly but inside he was leaping for joy. 'What quick reflexes' he thought. 'There's no stopping me now!'

Justin's fourth ball of the over (or third ball, not counting the 'dead ball') was short, again outside the off-stump. Mike slashed again trying to repeat his last shot. He mis-timed it, got a thick edge and the ball flew over gully's head. There was no third man — so four runs again!

More generous applause from the spectators and more self-congratulations between the batsmen contrasted against a background of thunderous glares from Justin, first at his skipper for apparently deliberately failing to have a third man to take the catch, and then at Spaghetti for having the nerve to hit him for successive fours. Justin shook his head sadly. He couldn't remember ever having had such bad luck. Everyone and everything was conspiring against him! Well, he'd show them! Justin's next two balls were dynamite.

The first flew off a length and got a thin outside edge to second slip who dropped a sharp chance, probably by standing too close to the wicket. The second cut in, this time found the inside edge of the bat and passed safely right across the face of the stumps past the finer of the two backward-short-legs and sped towards the undefended fine-leg boundary. A Chinese late cut for four!

One more ball remained in the first over, Justin's seventh. One more incident and this over would have to get in the 'Guinness Book of Records' thought Justin — as the most eventful, most unlucky over ever bowled by an opening bowler.

'Just my luck' whined Justin. 'Just my flipping luck to have a half-wit for a brother who hasn't a clue how to set a decent field, fielders who couldn't catch to save their lives and a batsman who has more lives than my gran's cat, Tiddler! Just my flipping luck!'

Somehow Justin pulled himself together for one final effort that over.

Justin pulled himself together for one final effort that over.

The ball beat the bat and struck the pad hard.

If the previous two balls were just too good for Mike then this ball was simply unplayable. It pitched on a length outside off stump and cut in wickedly. Mike just had time to stick his front foot well-down the wicket outside the line of the off-stump and attempt a forward defensive shot, bat and pad together, head over the ball, left elbow high. The ball beat the bat and struck the pad hard. It bounced into the eager hands of silly mid-off who held the ball aloft in his outstretched hand as he turned towards the umpire claiming a bat-and-pad-catch; Justin wheeled around in the middle of his follow-through and jump-turned to face the umpire and joined with the wicket-keeper in a soul-shattering appeal for LBW; the entire slip cordon stretched their hands to heaven and claimed anything and everything!

It bounced into the eager hands of silly mid-off.

It needed a strong and wise umpire to resist such an orchestrated and confident appeal. But Mr Able, Mike's English teacher and deputy headmaster, was indeed such a man.

He was unmoved.

He was unimpressed.

He took a little time to consider the appeal and decided against it. He was sure the ball had missed the bat, that the batsman had tried to play the ball and that, although the ball was cutting in and would quite probably have gone on to hit the wicket, it had struck the pad outside the line of the off-stump.

Mr Able shook his head firmly in a negative fashion, tossed his last pebble high in the air by way of transferring it from his right to his left hand, pocketed it, calmly announced, 'Over' and had practically walked all the way to square leg for the start of the next over before the hysteria in the slips had died down.

Fourteen runs had been taken off the first over without loss. Mike had lived dangerously but he had survived. He wiped the sweat of honest endeavour off his forehead while he reflected on his good shots and his close calls. *The Plan* was working well; runs were flowing and Justin was losing his rag. You need a little luck in cricket and Mike felt it was going to be his day!

Chapter Four

Spider Spadcock could barely contain himself. He had yet to face his first ball and couldn't wait to get into the action.

On the basis that Kynaston could have taken three or four wickets in the first over, their skipper Adrian kept to his aggressive field with his second opening bowler, Chris Pailer.

The square-leg umpire, 'Twiggy' Kemp, was now at the bowler's end for the second over and after giving Spider his guard (leg stump) he announced the bowler's action: 'Left-arm-over.' Spider didn't care who was bowling or what he was bowling. He was itching to have a swing and see if he could equal Spaghetti's fourteen runs scored in the first over.

Chris Pailer was a dour, stocky bowler with an ungainly run-up. He was only medium-paced and tended to bowl 'chest-on', but he had big shoulders, which he used effectively to seam the ball both ways and he could place the ball on the spot more often than not. He was built like an ox and was the team's stock bowler, going on for up to twenty overs without a rest, rather than a fast strike bowler like Justin.

Spider thought that medium-paced bowling was meat and drink to him.

He swung gloriously at all six balls.

He failed to connect with the first five and was caught off the sixth.

Spider couldn't come to grips with the slanting ball a left-hand over-the-wicket bowls. The balls were moving diagonally from leg to off and Spider was swinging down the wrong line and failing to get anywhere near them. Moreover, Spider was not used to facing the new ball and the shine and seam were causing the ball to move about more than he could cope with.

At the other end, Mike could see exactly what was happening. After the fifth air shot Mike walked up the wicket and gave Spider some advice.

'Move your left shoulder round to the left Spider so you're facing the line of the ball. Open up your stance — you'll find it easier. Move over to a centre guard.'

Spider did as he was told, and sure enough he made contact but only by the thinnest of thin edges which went safely and surely to first slip.

The umpire, Twiggy, was undecided. He was nearing retirement age as the senior Physics teacher at Kynaston school and his

Spider knew he had touched the ball with his bat so he 'walked'.

hearing and eyesight were in a state of acute decline.

Spider, although usually quick-tempered, was nothing if not honest. He knew he had touched the ball because he felt it strike the edge of the bat so he 'walked' instantly thus saving an embarrassing situation.

Even the hard-headed Kynaston lot were moved to give Spider a polite round of applause for his good sportmanship — although this was poor consolation for Spider who had wanted to make the most of his opening opportunity.

It was the end of the over and the score stood at 14 for one. Simon 'Poser' Sheerman arrived at the wicket jauntily. He was at the non-striking end and looking forward to testing himself against Justin. The number three bat is often the best bat in the side: he needs to be able to play defensively if a wicket's fallen early on, or to be able to force the pace (if scoring has been slow), and to be able to play opening bowlers and spin bowlers equally well. Simon was just such a batsman. He was technically perfect, had received many hours of professional coaching, and wanted to make cricket his career. His easy-going, happy-go-lucky approach to life disguised a very serious commitment to the game and he was absolutely determined to distinguish himself.

Simon had a good eye. He could pick the ball up very early in its flight and would be quite capable of hitting his first ball, not for four, but six, straight back over the bowler's head. Mike knew this and resolved to give Simon the strike as quickly as possible. He had a quick word with the new batsman before he faced Justin again.

'Simon, there's a huge gap in front of the wicket. I'm going to push the first ball that's pitched up to me straight back down the wicket and I want you to come like the wind. Be ready, back-up properly and we'll have no trouble. Let's try to regain the initiative we had in the first over.'

Simon nodded in agreement. The first ball was indeed pitched up and Mike pushed forward as promised. The ball was passing Justin's right side as he veered over to the left in his follow through. Simon scampered down the wicket and Mike responded.

So far everything was going according to plan.

Then Justin stuck out a huge boot and somehow deflected the ball on to the non-striker's wicket. Of course Simon was well out

Justin stuck out a huge boot and somehow deflected the ball on to the non-striker's wicket.

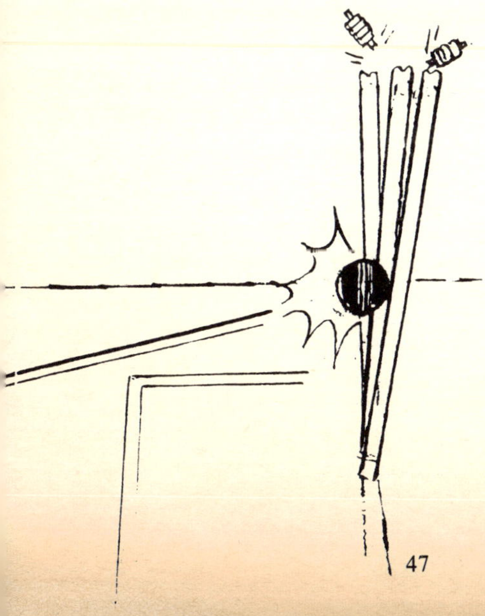

of his ground; he hadn't yet crossed with Mike so it was Simon that was given out by a couple of yards, by Mr Able.

For the first time that afternoon, Justin smiled.

'I can do anything with that right foot!' he said flicking the ball off the ground and into his hand with the foot in question. Justin was Kynaston's striker in their football first team and he did indeed have a deadly right boot although he didn't dream it would come in useful on the cricket pitch!

Simon shook his head sadly all the way back to the pavilion. He had not even faced a ball and would need a lot of consolation from his girlfriend Sue before he would be his usual chirpy self again. Oswestry was a mixed school and Sue was one of his classmates. Although she did not understand the game, she was prepared to hang around endlessly with her girlfriend Lynne waiting for Simon to share his moments of triumph and disaster with her, when he wasn't actually playing or practising. Sue was as pretty as Simon was handsome and when things went well they were a fine pair. When things went badly and Simon had a small sulk, Sue did her best to cheer him up but she thought the whole game was rather pointless and couldn't wait for Simon to grow up and grow out of these childish pursuits.

'The Crab' Mosey came in at number four.

'Hard luck Poser', Crab muttered to an obviously distressed Simon as their paths

Simon would need a lot of consoling from his girlfriend Sue, before he would be his usual chirpy self again.

crossed on his way to the wicket.

Kynaston had their tails up by this time and Crab, or Crabby as his friends called him, could feel the atmosphere thicken up as he approached the wicket from the outskirts of the pavilion. By the time he reached the wicket he could have sliced the atmosphere with his bat, it was so heavy and dripping with emotion. This Kynaston lot wanted to win badly and everyone was geeing everyone else up.

Again the new batsman was at the non-striker's end so Crab had to be content with watching Mike face the next ball from Justin.

Mike was feeling really bad about the run-out. It wasn't his fault, it was just one big fluke really, but he couldn't help feeling responsible somehow.

Justin roared in and Mike played a terrible cross-batted shot in a vain attempt to pull the ball to leg. In his state of mind, Mike would probably have played that particular shot whatever Justin had bowled. A batsman cannot afford to lose his concentration, not even for one ball, and Mike payed the penalty in full. He got a thick edge which ballooned straight up towards short leg.

'Mine' called the 'keeper as he charged up from his deep position behind the stumps. 'Fingers' Davis had a fine pair of hands. Like Justin, he played football but in goal, and with the help of his gloves he made no mistake in catching the ball.

Mike got a thick edge which ballooned straight up towards short leg.

'Fingers' Davis made no mistake in catching the ball.

Mike made a token attempt to run and with the ball in the air a long time, he managed to cross with Crabby giving him the strike next ball.

'Right that's it. End of Plan!' Pete pushed Beefy to one side as he promoted himself to number five in the batting order.

'Three quick wickets down and that's enough. We can't afford to lose any more. I'll shut up shop and expect you to do the same when you join me Beefy.'

Pete marched to the wicket. After the first over of the match his spirit had soared. His team mates had clapped him on the back, he had felt inspired, a genius even. But after the first over it had been all downhill. In less than three overs he had experienced the full range of human emotion from elation to despair. How he wished he had never dreamed up that awful Plan. Pete cursed the day, or rather night, he thought of it.

'O.K. that's it. We've had our little bit of fun and now we're going to be dead serious. Dead bat everything on the wicket.

Don't play anything off the wicket. We'll have to stick it out until Justin gets tired and gets taken off.' Pete issued his instructions to an attentive Mosey.

The Crab liked to play defensively and take his time to build a big innings, so it was no sweat for him. He faced the next four balls resolutely enough and kept his wicket intact.

Pete did likewise during the following over

and played out another maiden.

At the end of the fourth over, Oswestry had still only scored 14 runs and they had lost three wickets. They were still in big trouble although Pete and Crabby looked safe enough.

Justin put everything he had into the fifth over of the match, his third. He had warmed up, his team were decidedly on top and he was bowling as quickly and as well as he had ever done in his young life.

The Crab faced up to the challenge, fending off short deliveries and dropping his wrists at the moment of contact to keep the ball down. But this wasn't really getting Oswestry anywhere. No runs were coming off the bat and just one false move would lead to another vital wicket. Sure enough Crabby made that inevitable mistake, if you could call it that, that very over. On the fifth ball Justin banged the ball in fast and hard, managing to get a little more lift than usual, even on this near perfect wicket. With so many fielders in catching positions, poor Crab couldn't keep the ball down. He played a sort of leg glance, a reaction shot since the ball 'popped' up viciously, and he didn't have time to guide it with care and precision. Backward-short-leg took a superb catch as the ball sped by high on his left side.

'He stuck out a thumb — and pulled out a plum and said "What a good boy am I!" ' chanted Justin who was pleased, delighted and amazed that one of his team mates had actually managed to catch a ball in earnest.

Kynaston were by now cock-a-hoop.

Justin and Adrian were dancing around in an embrace of brotherly love which their parents had never witnessed during their entire upbringing. The rest of the Kynaston team had formed a circle around the Smith brothers and were egging them on with cheers and handclaps.

Justin and Adrian danced around in delight.

Pete hurried out to meet Beefy half-way to the wicket, glancing up at the scoreboard as he did so. Fourteen for four, last man 0.
Pete groaned.

'We need to dig in, Beefy. We need to dig in,' Pete entreated his huge easy-going friend earnestly.

Beefy just grinned. He only knew one way to play and that was to play every ball on its merits — and, as far as he knew, he'd never played a good ball in his life!

Pete scuttled alongside Beefy trying to keep up with his giant strides, gesticulating caution and begging him for his sake, for the school's sake and for the greater glory of mankind please to play sensibly on just this one occasion.

Beefy nooded to everything Pete said since he didn't want to upset his skipper, and, indeed, a large part of Beefy wanted to do the right thing for the First Team.

'Yes, sure, sure. You can count on me,' he found himself saying, but when Beefy got to the wicket his will power crumbled.

He looked around the field, at all the close fielders and instead of feeling intimidated he called over to the Kynaston skipper, 'Here mate are you serious? I can't be held responsible if I put your players in hospital. They're standing much too close to me — especially this little one here!' He prodded forward-short-leg in the stomach with the end of his bat and continued, 'I'll eat you for breakfast my little one!'

The Kynaston players looked perplexed. This

sort of behaviour in this sort of situation just did not add up. Kynaston were right on top. Didn't this great, big muscle-bound giant understand what a fix he was in? Adrian shrugged his shoulders. 'Let him have it, kid' he said to his brother Justin as he threw him the ball to finish off that over.

Beefy settled down in his crease to face the last ball of the over and to show these young boys that cricket is a man's game.

Chapter Five

Wham! Bang! Wallop!

Beefy had found his range! But not before he had given fleeting hope to the wicket keeper and first slip after an airy swipe that somehow failed to get an edge, and only just in time to save the final drop of blood from draining away from his skipper's ashen-grey face.

Pete could not believe his eyes. Had he not just impressed on his friend the dire circumstances they were in? Had he not advised caution? Had Beefy not agreed with every word that he had said?

Pete felt betrayed. This was a serious situation, and Beefy was treating it like a Sunday School outing. The honour of the School was at stake, and Beefy was behaving incredibly irresponsibly.

Pete tried to show his disapproval but could not manage to catch Beefy's eye. At the end of the over Pete had marched purposefully across to Beefy to try to drum some sense into him, but Beefy made no attempt to meet him at mid-wicket, being quite content to lean nonchalantly on his bat and gaze happily and abstractedly into the far distance, seemingly oblivious to all pressure and savouring the full flavour of a lovely summer afternoon.

Pete tried to show his disapproval but could not manage to catch Beefy's eye.

'Oh, what's the use!' shrugged Pete. 'He'll have to learn the hard way. I'm not wasting any more emotion on the big fellow. If he wants to throw his wicket away, then that's up to him. I've done my level best, I can't do more. Who does he think he is — Nelson? — the way he's turning a blind eye on me, pretending he can't see that I want a word with him!'

Pete was annoyed, and when it was his turn to face the bowling he took it out on the bowler.

Crash! Bang! Wallop!

Before he knew it, Pete was behaving as irresponsibly as Beefy! The ball was speeding to the boundary on all sides of the pitch. The score was mounting by leaps and bounds. Gradually Pete's anger turned to controlled aggression and he allowed himself the occasional smile as he savoured a particularly well-struck boundary.

Things were getting progressively easier at the wicket. The batsmen were getting their eyes in and playing with great confidence; the bowlers were getting tired and disheartened. The field had slowly been adjusted so that the accent had been changed from attack to defence — from primarily looking to get the batsman out to chiefly stopping them from scoring.

The slips had been reduced from three to one, with second slip dropping back to third man and third slip to extra cover; point was now deepish cover; silly mid-off now a very conventional mid-off; forward-short-leg moved to mid-on; one of the backward-short-legs was now at deep-square-leg and the other at fine leg.

The difference in the style of the two batsmen was quite marked.

Pete was looking for the gaps in the field and meticulously placing the ball in those gaps with a surgeon's precision.

Beefy's aim was to hit the ball out of the ground.

Beefy, on the other hand, wasn't worried about the fielders. His aim was to hit the ball over the fielders, over the boundary, and preferably out of the ground. The ball did not always go in the direction he aimed it, so it was impossible to set a field to him, although to the eternal credit of the Kynaston skipper every attempt was made to stem the flow of the runs. Justin took himself off when he found himself getting such rough treatment, and Adrian could not persuade him to try a second spell later, even though he pleaded. No less than six different bowlers were used in quick succession, and every blade of grass had been covered at one time or another by one of Adrian's fielders

Adrian tried to set a field to Beefy but it was an impossible job.

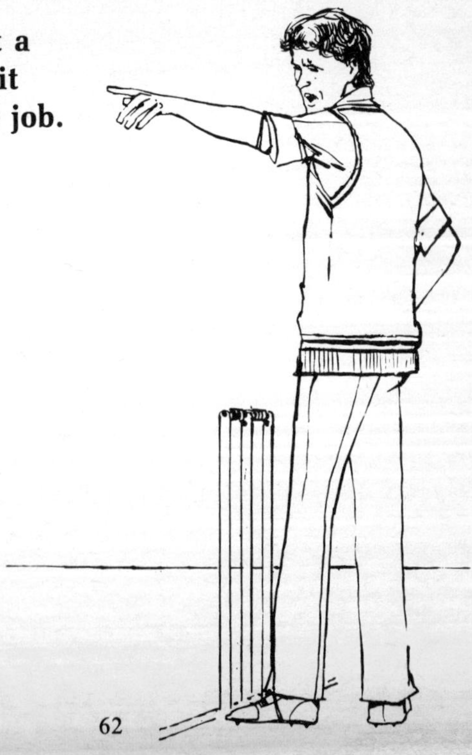

— but somehow the ball always bounced tantalizingly out of reach.

Beefy was playing some exceptional shots; they must have been exceptional because they certainly weren't in the book! But he was living dangerously. It was surely only a matter of time before he would give a chance or two and, true enough, that's exactly what happened.

The first chance went to cover.

The ball was still rising as it passed cover's right ear. He struck out a hand only to see the

The cover fielder stuck out a hand only to see the top joint of his first finger break.

top joint of first finger break and bend sidways as he deflected the ball fractionally on its inevitable way to the boundary. The cover fielder was led off the field with a permanent reminder of the force of Beefy's hitting.

After that, the fielders seemed to rather avoid getting in the way of the ball. Suddenly, they all developed slow reactions, only lurching at balls once they had safely passed by, or finding it incredibly difficult to 'pick the ball up' out of the background. Many a fielder was to be seen running in completely the wrong direction, squinting madly and feigning surprise at the distance they had managed to put between themselves and the ball.

Justin sulked in the outfield and did not even make a pretence of chasing any balls.

The second chance went to long-off.

He should have been standing on the boundary, but had crept in a little way, and when he found the ball ballooning towards him he got excited and took a further couple of steps in. It is difficult to judge a long distance ball which is coming to you. Will it drop short, or will it fly over your head? Deep square-leg, at right angles to the trajectory of the ball, could see exactly where the ball would land but poor long-off had to sweat it out, and should have resisted the temptation to run in too soon. As he was about to find out, it's much easier to make a catch running forward, if you've misjudged it, than to take it over your shoulder with your back to the ball, running away from the wicket.

Long-off froze at the moment he realized that the ball was going to clear him. Back-pedalling wildly, he threw his right arm out high and wide as the ball passed overhead and, miraculously, the ball stuck!

Back-pedalling wildly, he threw his right arm out high and wide and miraculously the ball stuck.

Long-off had the ball in his hands, but he wasn't quite in control of the situation. His forward momentum had been rapidly changed first to a backward one, and then upwards and sideways as he leapt to catch the ball, and although he managed to avoid falling over he was spinning and weaving across the grass like an ice-skater.

Furthermore, the elation he felt at taking such an important and spectacular catch added an extra spring to his step and he ended up taking at least a dozen additional unnecessary giant leaping steps as he partly tried to regain his balance and partly celebrated his good fortune. Unfortunately for him, his out-of-control, curving run took him at one point over the boundary, and the umpire ruled that the ball, although caught, was not entirely under control at the moment he crossed the line, and instead of claiming a victim, poor long-off had given away a six!

Beefy had already started walking towards the pavilion, and half the fielding side were galloping towards long-off to join him in his victory run when the umpire announced his decision.

Well, that really knocked the stuffing out of Kynaston. If they were dispirited before, then this incident pushed them over the edge of despair. They moved listlessly around the field and failed to respond to their skipper's frequent appeals of 'Come on fellows! Heads up! One final effort — Let's have one final effort!'

Fielding errors multiplied; ones turned into twos, twos into threes and over-throws were commonplace as fielders failed to back-up wild throw-ins.

Fielders failed to back up wild throw-ins as the fielding errors multiplied.

The once popular Kynaston skipper was now aware that he had lost a grip on the game. His colleagues who, only half an hour earlier, had been singing his praises, were muttering darkly behind his back about what he should be doing to save the situation. But he had tried everything. The only solution was to stick to it, play as well as they could, and like, Micawber, hope that something would turn up.

The whole nature of the game had changed from bowler versus batsman to batsman versus batsman, as both Pete and Beefy tried to 'farm' the bowling and outscore each other.

It was jamboree time! Every ball was a free gift, every free gift was eagerly accepted by Pete and Beefy and noisily acclaimed by the First Team's delirious supporters on the boundary.

Biff!! Bang!! Wallop!!

Chapter Six

At tea Pete found himself trying to placate Beefy. He was trying to explain his somewhat surprising early declaration when the score had reached 129 for 4. Beefy just could not understand why someone would want to put a stop to something so beautiful. 'It was like poetry in motion, man' Beefy was saying. 'There was no way they were going to get us out. We should have built up the score so big that they would have run out of numbers in the score book! We should have kept hitting them so hard that they begged for mercy and got down on their bended knees and surrendered.'

Pete would have laughed if he hadn't thought Beefy was absolutely serious. 'Cricket doesn't work like that, Beefy. If you score too many runs the opposition gives up trying to win and settles for a draw instead. I want all the time I can get to winkle Kynaston out. I'm not prepared to settle for a draw, or give Kynaston a chance of forcing one. Believe me, Kynaston are demoralised and we'll get them out for less than 80. You'll see.'

The Oswestry team were all sitting together at a long tressle table set some distance apart from Kynaston. Everyone was listening to Pete's conversation with Beefy, so Pete took the opportunity of having a quick word with the First Team over tea instead of in the changing room later.

'Well team, my Plan didn't quite work the way I meant it to — but we got to where we wanted to by tea didn't we? We're bang on schedule for a great win. My thanks to the early batsmen who obeyed orders and committed suicide and to Beefy for being as pig-headed as ever! That's just about the finest knock I've seen from you Beefy! How many balls did you lose?'

'Two. And I was only just warming up when you . . .'

'Yes. Well thank you Beefy. I don't think we want to go into all that again! We've got quite enough runs. Beefy got his 50 and then some so we should all be well-satisfied. Let's press home our advantage and get the wickets we need to win. Remember we only need to take 9 wickets because poor Chopper Johnson's broken his finger trying to hold onto one of Beefy's great heaves, silly fellow, and he won't be batting.

'O.K. Enough said. Just don't eat too much tea because we still have some work to do!'

The team spirit was good so Pete had an

easy task between innings. His main job would be out on the field, keeping up those spirits and making sure that Kynaston wickets fell with monotonous regularity.

Pete was in a bold mood today. All season he had approached each game with reasonable caution, playing carefully and not taking unnecessary risks with his captaincy. Now, in the most important match of all, he had thrown caution to the wind.

His original Plan had been bold enough. Now he was improvising and responding to the situation as he saw it and he resolved to be equally bold in the second half of the match.

The gusting wind had given them little trouble when they were batting but during tea the wind had picked up and Pete wanted to see whether he could make some use of it before it blew itself out.

Also, the sun was almost directly behind the bowlers' arm at the classroom end of the wicket and although it was a little high at present, it would soon descend to an interesting position where it might give the batsmen a little trouble later on. Pete was nothing if not observant!

'Right Crabby I want you to open the bowling at the classroom end. Throw the ball up high, give it plenty of air. I want to tempt these Kynaston openers into a series of indiscretions!'

'The Crab' looked surprised. 'Pete must have hidden depths,' he thought. First he opens the batting with his best fast bowler. That's surprising enough. But now he opens his bowling with his slowest bowler! Crabby thought he knew his skipper well — but evidently he didn't know him at all! 'The man's either a genius or an idiot,' thought Crabby, but who was he to complain? He loved bowling and that's what the skipper wanted him to do so let battle commence!

The Kynaston openers had had an easy season. The entire side had not been required to score more than 100 runs all season. Justin had been so successful that 70 or 80 runs had been enough to seal victory. On one famous occasion, 25 runs had done the job when Justin had skittled out an entire side almost single-handed in just 10 overs, finishing with 8 wickets for 10 runs!

Consequently, the Kynaston openers had not really had to apply themselves all season. They were in an unfamiliar situation and were no longer feeling especially confident about winning. Their captain had not bothered to give them a proper team talk during the interval because he felt he hadn't received the support he wanted in the field. He'd just told them they 'were a shower' and to get on with it and see if they could bat better than they had bowled, which shouldn't be difficult in his opinion, he said.

Since they'd been left to their own devices, the openers decided to take a good look at the bowling and not to hurry things along.

They'd imagined that they would be facing a couple of fast bowlers so when the Crab came on to bowl they were a little surprised. The wicketkeeper, Andy, was standing right up, the field was spread out and the bowler took a fairly short run. Not at all what the openers were used to and not to their liking at all!

'Play' called umpire Mable and the Kynaston innings had begun.

The Crab began his run-up and suddenly it became very clear where he got his nickname from. He sort of sidled up to the wicket in a disjointed fashion, every one of his limbs seeming to be in opposition to the others. His was not a smooth run-up that started slowly and ended up fast. Rather, it was a jerky affair, first fast then slow, then fast and slow again. All the time the right shoulder was flexing up and down as if the bowler was preparing to release the ball at any moment. The style may have been ridiculous (and spectators had been known to collapse in laughter) but it certainly was effective. Because with this action, the Crab was able to spin prodigious leg-breaks and googlies. Good leg-break bowlers are few and far between in any class of cricket, let alone school cricket. So Crabby always had a surprise factor in his favour. The batsmen were not used to facing good spin bowling and certainly couldn't spot his googly.

The opening batsmen could hardly stick to their plan of playing cautiously when they were faced with Crabby's bowling. In the first place it was difficult to block this type of bowling and in the second place it looked as though it ought

Crabby

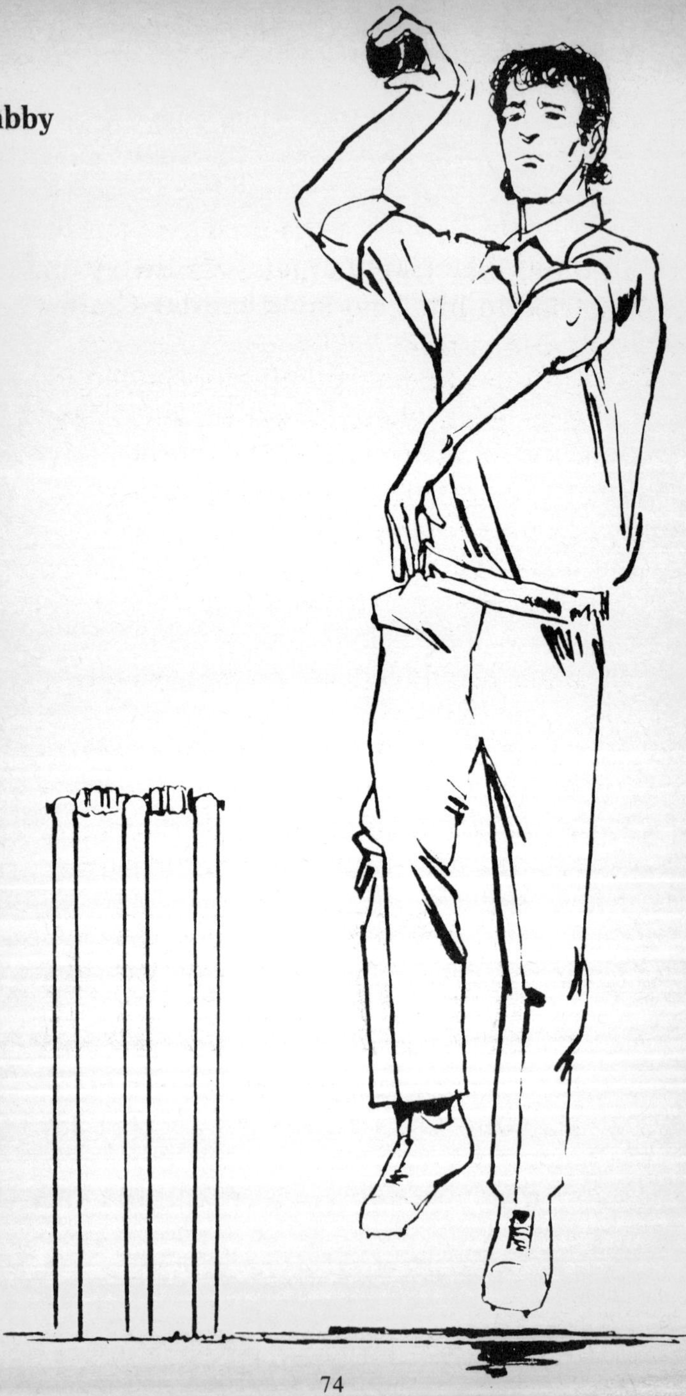

to be hit — it looked very friendly indeed.

Crabby had a great first over. He made the openers look like a couple of court jesters who had been sent to amuse the King and his courtiers. First they tried to play defensively and then they tried to hit. They tried to play Crabby from the crease and then they tried to move their feet — but the flight and the breeze made things difficult when the ball was in the air and the batsmen went charging out only to be deceived by the flight of the ball and to end up racing back to their crease to prevent themselves being stumped.

The first over brought many laughs but no wickets.

Poser Sheerman bowled left arm leg-breaks at the other end, so it was an all-spin attack Pete was using. Poser used the wind to advantage as well, although he didn't spin the ball very much, if at all. He had a beautifully smooth run-up, delivered the ball side-on in perfect text-book manner and fielded brilliantly to his own bowling.

Once again, the openers had difficulty in playing spin and it would surely only be a question of time before the wickets began to fall.

First one opener and then the other was caught in the deep, both choosing to hit against the spin from the Crab, with disasterous results. Deep mid-wicket picked up one catch and long leg the other.

Poser got the next two wickets, one a stumping by his good mate, Andy, the other an

LBW decision that had the batsman playing for a non-existant spin. 'That was my arm ball' Simon proudly boasted while Pete and Mike exchanged knowing winks.

The stumping had given Poser particular pleasure. He had tossed the ball up higher than ever, had bowled it from 23 metres and flighted it with tremendous top spin. The wind and the batsman did the rest, leaving his 'keeper the easiest of stumpings. Looking at the stranded batsman well out of his ground, Poser felt the elation that a top class tennis player feels when he plays a masterful disguised lob that leaves his aggressive opponent flat-footed at the net.

All the time the score was mounting steadily. There was the occasional full toss, eagerly despatched to the leg-side boundary and the odd long-hop which got similar treatment. The wind did indeed blow itself out and there was a nasty period for Pete when the bowlers were not making much headway and the runs were flowing a little too easily.

Pete did not want to close the game up so he resisted bringing on the fast bowlers. He persisted with his slow bowlers and marked time until the setting sun manoeuvred itself into the desired position behind the Crab's arm. Crabby altered his action to round-the-wicket to use the sun as early as possible; then as the sun dropped and moved around, he switched back to over-the-wicket to get a second bite at the sun's helpful rays.

The score was 56 for 4 when Crabby

Crabby switched to round-the-wicket.

switched to round-the-wicket and Kynaston were looking good. Five overs later, three from the Crab, and the game was nearly over! The Crab was virtually unplayable. The ball was lofted into the sun and was not seen again by the batsmen. Four wickets fell in this short time, all clean-bowled or LBW. Several chances went begging behind the wicket since the wicket-keeper and slip were also affected by the sun and couldn't see any better than the batsmen themselves. The umpire, however, had his back to the sun and had no difficulty in giving LBW decisions.

When the eighth wicket fell with the score on 68, Oswestry thought for a moment that they had won. The number 10 batsman failed to arrive at the wicket, number 11 had not returned from hospital and the players were about to leave the field when Justin appeared, somewhat reluctantly. He was dressed in jeans and sneakers with his shirt hanging out of his jeans. One pad had been hastily strapped on by his team-mates who also had to frog-march him to the wicket. Apparently, Justin had had enough of the game, had changed and was slinking off home when his brother had caught him and, with a little help, forced him to bat.

Pete could have claimed the match under the two minute rule but he didn't want to win in that despicable way. He didn't make a fuss about the long delay.

'Justin time' chanted the Kynaston supporters in relief when they realised they

Justin didn't seem to care if Kynaston won or lost.

were still in the game with a chance, albeit a slim one.

The sun was no longer behind the bowler's arm, so Justin at least was spared this indignity. Justin didn't even take a guard. He held his bat up high in the air, in the modern style, like England opener Gooch, and swung at everything.

Justin had nothing to lose. He didn't seem to care if Kynaston won or lost. His day had already been spoilt by the way his bowling had been treated. He was a proud lad and he had not expected to receive such harsh treatment. It was enough to make him think seriously about packing in the game. Justin was only interested in things that came easily to him so if he couldn't be a star without effort, he'd rather opt out all together.

Poser and the Crab bowled at Justin expecting little resistance. But Justin batted like a tennis player who was match-point down. He'd got nothing to lose so he went for broke. No tensions, no inhibitions obstructed his play. His arrogance was untouched by his recent failure with the ball and his timing was immaculate because, after all, he was a natural ball-player. Balls sped to all corners of the field. Justin was a selfish person and a selfish bat. He found no difficulty in farming the bowling and only allowed his partner, young Sid Goings, the occasional ball.

Before Pete knew what was happening, the score had miraculously reached 120 for 8. Justin had scored a quicker 50 than Beefy and looked set to end up the hero of the match after all, although not quite in the way he had anticipated.

Pete held a hurried conference with his vice-skipper Mike.

They agreed that Beefy should be tried. He was always full of surprises and the First Team needed someone who could pull a rabbit out of a hat. But Justin was no rabbit and Pete threw the ball to Beefy with a heavy heart. It was his first bowling change of the match and this could be the last over, one way or the other. What a creature of extremes he was being today!

In retrospect, Pete felt that he should have changed the bowling earlier, but who would have thought Justin capable of this type of innings?

'Thought he was supposed to be a bowler' muttered Pete darkly to himself as he braced himself for probable defeat.

'Whether 'tis nobler in the mind to suffer
the slings and arrows of outrageous fortune,'

Pete was wallowing in self-pity and turned to Shakespeare again for solace as he set the field for Beefy's first over.

Beefy was feeling altogether confident. He couldn't understand why he hadn't been called on before and knew this was a time to be optimistic. He overheard his skipper's morose mutterings and rejoined:

'Or to take arms against a sea of troubles,
And by opposing end them?'

Umpire Mable, deputy headmaster and head of English had done a fine job in educating the First Team!

'You're right, Beefy! Let's finish this game off!' Pete's black mood lifted. Beefy had entirely misunderstood Hamlet's suicidal speech and had turned it into something positive! Pete had to laugh. Perhaps Beefy could turn the game after all!

Chapter Seven

Beefy grabbed the ball from Pete and glowered at Justin.

Justin glowered at Beefy.

The two potential match-winners squared up to each other. Nothing was said, but volumes were spoken!

Beefy broke the spell by snorting contemptuously and marching back to the start of his run-up, which was a good twelves paces behind the wicket. Beefy bowled fastish right-arm-over seamers. His action was conventional but his deliveries were anything but! Beefy liked to experiment, to try different types of balls — to probe at a batsman's defences and to find out his weaknesses. He wasn't a great student in class but was an intuitive master of this game; somehow he usually did the right thing, without ever knowing why.

Beefy loved to rise to the occasion and there

was no doubt in his mind as he rushed in to deliver his first ball that he was about to win the game for the First Team.

But Justin had not read the script which Beefy had prepared for him. He was in a mean mood and swatted the ball bad-temperedly like the school bully he undoubtedly was. The ball went scurring to the boundary like one of Justin's tormented juniors trying to escape him in the school playground.

124 runs for 8 wickets!

The situation was getting desperately close, yet Beefy and Justin continued to play with utter disregard to the gravity of the circumstances they found themselves in.

Justin showed no enjoyment in scoring his last boundary. A thunderous cloud seemed to hover just above his head and he seemed intent only on trying to part the leather on the ball from its cork and string interior.

Beefy experimented with balls two and three, the first of which slipped out of his hand and whizzed full toss past Justin's head — a beamer! Justin barely moved, just swayed gently back, rocking on his heels and letting the ball pass very close to his nose. It would take more than this to make him lose his cool. The second experimental ball, Beefy's third, was wide down the leg-side. Umpire Twiggy Kemp did not signal a wide. Justin apparently thought otherwise and indicated as much by stretching out his hands and signalling direct to the scorers. The umpire was not amused.

Ball number five was well pitched up and Justin hit it straight back over Beefy's head. It was four runs all the way.

Pete's heart was thudding noisily and busily under his sweater. He was the captain but he felt so helpless watching these two goliaths duelling.

128 for 8! only two runs wanted by Kynaston. Pete gulped. This had gone far enough. Pete raced to Beefy's side.

'A yorker, Beefy! Bowl a yorker!' He entreated.

'What do you think I'm trying to do, Skip!!' Beefy looked hurt.

Pete shrugged and returned to his position at point.

He would have to carry the can for this defeat — it was no good blaming anyone else.

Beefy took an extra long run up for his next and fifth ball.

The day was drawing to a close and the evening light threw an uncanny shadow over the proceedings. To an outsider it looked as though a strange form of witchcraft was being practised; only the drumbeats were missing as Beefy thudded up to the wicket and bowled . . . a perfect yorker!

The ball flew into the block-hole. Justin had his bat up, Gooch-style, and for some reason did not bother to bring it down. The ball flew onto the stumps scattering them in all directions! The entire crowd around the ground erupted. Oswestry supporters were jubilant, the Kynaston supporters angry with disbelief. To all intents and purposes it looked as though Justin had thrown his wicket away.

To all the world it looked as though Justin had thrown the match; that he had shown everyone how easily he could have hit the winning run — but just couldn't be bothered, preferring to treat the game like a sick joke.

Justin was booed off the field. Beefy was carried off shoulder high.

Only Pete, at point, was close enough to see what really happened on that fateful last ball and he wasn't telling anybody. A swarm of midges had flown into Justin's eye at the crucial moment, obscuring his vision. Before he knew what had happened his stumps were levelled to the floor and the game was over. Oswestry had won by one run and Justin was too proud to tell anyone what had really happened — and who would believe him anyway? Certainly not Beefy! If people wanted to think he had thrown the match, let them, thought Justin. It was a silly game anyway!

Pete thought otherwise. As he sat reflecting on the game, sipping his soft drink at the reception laid on in the school hall after the game, he felt well-satisfied.

He would go down in the annals of school cricket as a famous and successful Captain and pupils would talk about his brave declaration and positive approach to the game for years to come.

But the ultimate winner was the game itself. What sort of game was it that could unfold so

Only Pete could see what had really happened on the last ball. A swarm of midges had flown into Justin's eye at the crucial moment.

many twists and turns, that could provide so many opportunities for glory and failure, that could hold so many secrets for the uninitiated, that could provide so much pleasure for participant and spectator alike?

'Yes' smiled Pete as he stretched out his legs, 'Cricket's the finest game on earth!'

And who would disagree with that?

Pete sat reflecting on the game, sipping a drink.

GLOSSARY

Beamer
A ball that is a fast full toss at head height.

Bouncer, bumper
A ball that is bowled short and fast, bouncing up off the pitch at head height.

Cut
Cuts are strokes played to balls that are short and wide of the off stump. The square cut involves a short of chopping action from a standing position. The late cut aims at steering the ball just behind the stumps on the off side.

Drives
The basic cricket shots are drives. The drive starts with a high backlift, swings down with a straight bat and follows through in the direction the ball is hit. Drives are usually hit along the ground. A straight drive is hit past the bowler, straight down the ground. A cover drive goes between extra cover and cover fielders.

Full toss
A ball that does not pitch at all before it reaches the batsman.

Glance
The glance is a little deflection of the ball down the leg side.

Leg side
The area of the field to the left of the batsman if he is righthanded is known as the leg side. The stump to his left nearest his legs is the leg stump.

Length
The length of the bowling is the spot on the pitch where the ball pitches or bounces. A good length ball has the batsman in two minds, whether to play back or come forward. A ball short of a length is generally easier to play, giving the batsman time to decide which shot he will use.

Long hop
A long hop is a ball that is very short and easy to hit because it comes right on to the batsman and gives him time to find his shot and hit the ball well.

Maiden over
An over in which no runs are scored.

Off side
The side of the field to the right of a righthanded batsman is known as the off side. The stump furthest away from the legs is the off stump.

Pull and hook
The pull and the hook are played against any short delivery that comes right at the batsman's body or in line with the stumps. The ball is hit across towards square leg.

Spin
In spin bowling the ball turns when it pitches. An off spinner bowling to a righthanded batsman turns the ball from the off to the leg side. While the leg spinner or leg break bowler spins the ball the opposite way.

Yorker
A ball that bounces right on the batsman's toes or just under his bat.

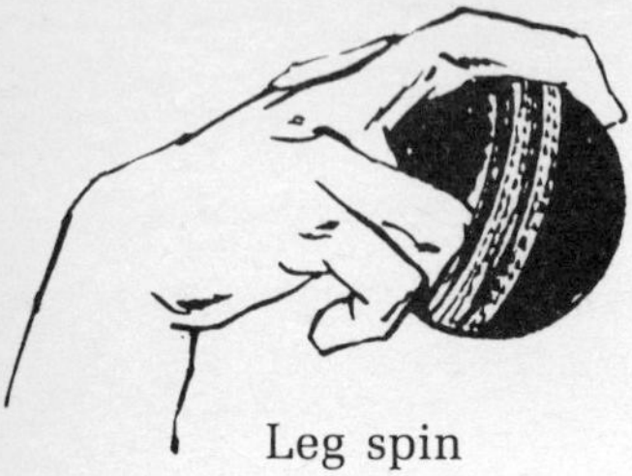

Leg spin

Leg cutter

Out swing

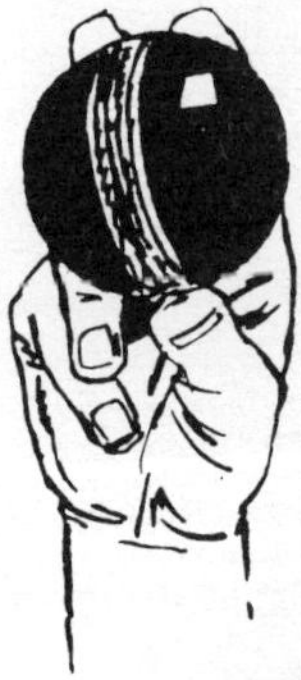

In swing

Off cutter

Off spin

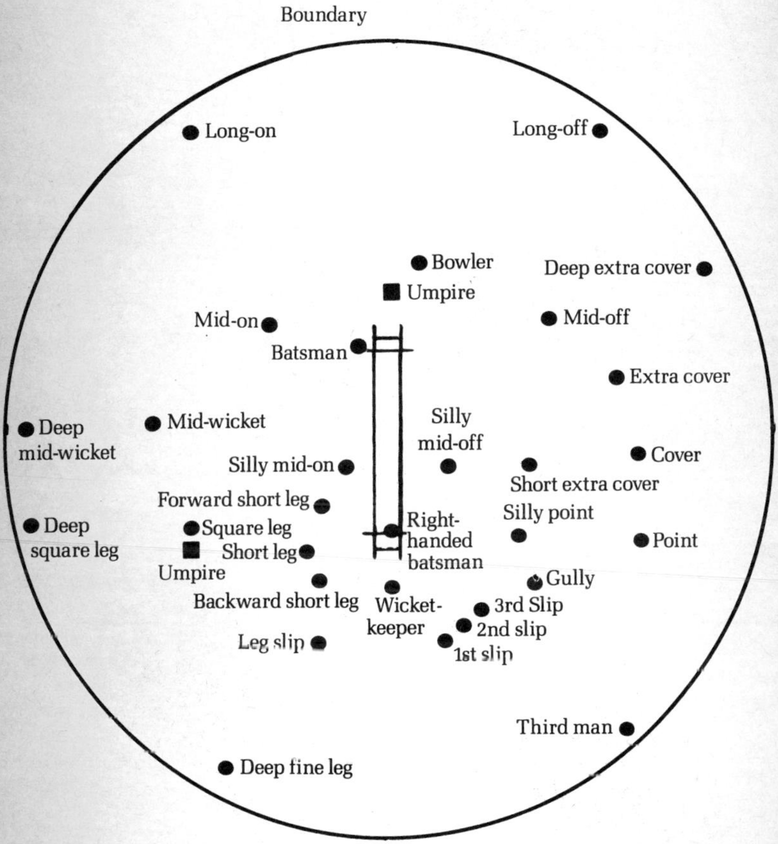
Boundary
Long-on
Long-off
Bowler
Deep extra cover
Umpire
Mid-on
Mid-off
Batsman
Extra cover
Deep mid-wicket
Mid-wicket
Silly mid-off
Silly mid-on
Cover
Short extra cover
Forward short leg
Silly point
Deep square leg
Square leg
Right-handed batsman
Point
Short leg
Umpire
Gully
Backward short leg
Wicket-keeper
3rd Slip
2nd slip
Leg slip
1st slip
Third man
Deep fine leg

About the Author

Peter Sackett, once a young school cricket captain himself, is now, by all accounts, nearing the end of his useful cricketing life although he protests that he is a late developer and is still improving. His remaining ambitions are small: to establish a regular place in The First Team at Tring Park Cricket Club where he enjoyed his best ever season last year amassing (too slowly, if his critics are to be believed) over 1200 runs, with two undefeated centuries.

Born in Patna, India, of English, Danish, French and Canadian descent, the author travelled widely throughout the riot-torn provinces of Sind and Kashmir during Partition with his Mother, a Red Cross Supervisor, before moving to newly-created Pakistan where he was educated briefly and intermittently at Karachi Grammar School, frequently playing truant to sail on Bunder boats in the Indian Ocean.

Further educated at Wolverton Grammar School, England, the author swapped a flying career in the Royal Air Force, where he helped navigate V-bombers as part of a five-man crew, for an undistinguished but mercurial career in book publishing.

His sports-loving schoolmaster Father, his gorgeous and talented wife Elisabeth, his beautiful daughters Charlotte and Hannah, together with the endless hours he spends occupying the crease in the cricket season, provide the author with the stability and relaxation that have helped him to recover from his unsettled but exotic early life.